Patrick Francis Moran

The St. Bartholomew Massacre August 24th, 1572

Patrick Francis Moran

The St. Bartholomew Massacre August 24th, 1572

ISBN/EAN: 9783337350789

Printed in Europe, USA, Canada, Australia, Japan

Cover: Foto ©ninafisch / pixelio.de

More available books at **www.hansebooks.com**

THE

ST. BARTHOLOMEW MASSACRE,

24th *AUGUST*, 1572.

———·———

PAPER

PRESENTED TO THE

Historical Society of St. Kieran's College,

MARCH, 1875,

BY

RIGHT REV. PATRICK F. MORAN,

Bishop of Ossory.

———

DUBLIN:

BROWNE & NOLAN, NASSAU-STREET.

1875.

THE

ST. BARTHOLOMEW MASSACRE.

THE 24th of August, 1572, marks a rubric festival in the annals of France, for it recalls a terrible deed of vengeance executed by the Court and by an outraged nation against the Huguenots. It is also a rubric feast in the calendar of those who assail the Catholic Church in this kingdom, whilst it affords a popular theme for declaiming against her persecuting spirit, for all the crimes and horrors of that bloody day are laid at the door of the Sovereign Pontiff, and of the Catholics of France. That no link might be wanting in the terrible accusation, the French infidels of the last century supplied an abundance of imaginary details, all of which were accepted without hesitation by the agents and abettors of the Protestant tradition of England. The words of Chenier were repeated in English pulpits—that the Cardinal de Lorraine had blessed the poignards of the assassins at the Louvre, and had given the signal for the massacre; it mattered but little that that illustrious Cardinal was, at the time, far away from France, not having as yet returned from Rome, whither he had gone to take part in the Conclave for the election of Pope Gregory the Thirteenth. The words of Voltaire were also accepted as historic truth—that the clergy were the active agents of this butchery, and that the assassins immolated their unhappy victims, wielding a dagger in one hand and holding a crucifix in the other; and yet it was well known that this wicked picture rested solely on the fancy of that prince of infidels, and proceeded from his diabolical hatred against the Catholic priesthood, and against the cross, the symbol of redemption.

Three years ago the second centenary of this massacre was not forgotten amongst us, and then these stories were once more eagerly repeated in the pulpit and in the press, with all the earnestness that Protestant fanaticism could inspire, and with such variety as each one's imagination could supply. The Westminster Abbey celebration merits to be specially referred to, though many would, perhaps, expect that at least the Dean of Westminster would be raised high above such prejudices : nevertheless, he availed himself of his sermon on that occasion to inform the British public that the massacre was perpetrated "with the express approbation" of the Sovereign Pontiff. A few years earlier, Froude, in his "History of England" (vol. x.), had pictured in minute detail all the particulars that could be imagined connected with that St. Bartholomew's feast, repeating the most childish tales regarding it. Since then the very same tales have once more found a place in his pages, whilst he accused the Catholics of Ireland of a premeditated massacre of their Protestant neighbours in the memorable year 1641. By such imaginative writers, the Catholics of France, accused of every crime, are painted in the darkest colours, and at the same time the harmless Huguenots are set before us in the light of peaceable citizens, only desirous of permission to practise the religion which they professed—innocent victims involved in sudden ruin by the fell, persecuting spirit and treacherous intolerance of Rome. And yet why should we complain of Voltaire, or Froude, or Dean Stanley, or the many other apostles of the Protestant tradition of England, when we find Lord Acton, and writers of his school, who, though professing the Catholic faith, yet seek to give the stamp of history to such calumnies, and to fan the flame of popular fanaticism against the Holy See, by accusing it of guilty complicity in this dreadful massacre ?

You will not expect, however, that in this short paper I would analyze, much less refute in detail, all the calumnies that have been uttered, and the misstatements that have been made on the subject of this St. Bartholomew's bloody festival. The task which I assume is a much simpler one—to present a brief but truthful narrative of the leading facts connected with that terrible day, and in doing so I will endeavour to arrange my remarks under the three following heads :—

First—The principal events connected with the Massacre :

Second—The causes of that widespread discontent which prompted so many persons throughout France to deeds of violence against the Huguenots:

Third—In fine, a few of the chief questions which have arisen regarding this festival of St. Bartholomew.

I.

During the first months of the year 1572, the policy of the French king and court was wholly favourable to the Huguenots. The leaders of the party were summoned to the capital ; many of the highest offices of state were intrusted to them, and every civil or religious privilege that they contended for was readily accorded them. In a most special manner dignities and honours were conferred on the Admiral Coligny, who was their ablest champion as well in council as in the field ; and, to crown all, the king, Charles IX., offered his sister in marriage to the young Prince Henry of Navarre, on whom the Huguenots had now centred all their hopes of securing for themselves one day the great prize of the diadem of France. This marriage, being contrary to the disciplinary laws of the Catholic Church, met with a stern and uncompromising opposition from the Holy See. Charles, however, persisted in his design, and in defiance of the most solemn repeated prohibitions, the marriage was celebrated in Paris with extraordinary pomp on the 18th of August, 1572.[1]

Walsingham was at this time English ambassador at the French court. In his despatches he gives free expression to the feelings of delight with which he witnessed this happy course of events, so favourable to the Huguenots, who were the open friends and secret allies of England. He does not, however, merely record the favours and privileges accorded to his friends ; he further attests that the king, being solely intent on enjoying the silly amusements of the court, was wholly guided by the counsels of Coligny ; and he even ventures to express a hope that ere long they would witness "the king's revolt from papistry."[2]

Catherine de Medici, the Queen Mother, was not one who would acquiesce without a struggle in the paramount influence thus acquired by the Huguenot leaders. She had long been their friend and patron, but now that they would seek to undermine her power, and set aside her authority, she became

---

[1] *White*, "Massacre of St. Bartholomew," page 358.
[2] See extracts from these despatches in Sir James Mackintosh's "History of England," iii., 220.

at once their most determined and most unscrupulous enemy.[1]
Charles the Ninth, her son, being only in his tenth year on his
accession to the throne of France, in 1560, Catherine, with
the approval of the Council of State, assumed the authority,
though without the title, of Regent; and even after the king
had attained his majority, she continued with supreme and
undisputed power to rule the kingdom. The Guises were at
first her only rivals, and as they were the recognised leaders
of the Catholic party, it became to her a matter of supreme
political interest to foster the restless followers of the reformed
tenets; and though she publicly avowed her resolve to administer justice with even balance to all the contending parties,
she never failed, when an opportunity presented itself, to throw
her protecting mantle over the Huguenots, and to sustain them
by all the influence which she could command. Catherine,
from her childhood, had imbibed the notorious principles of
Macchiavellian policy, which then held sway in the court of
Florence, and these were her only guide in the government
of France. It will, therefore, not surprise us to learn that for
a time the project was seriously entertained by her of adopting
the reformed tenets as the national religion,[2] for thus it was
hoped that the Catholic party would be inexorably crushed, and
that Protestant alliances would be secured for France against
the growing power and encroachments of Spain.[3] Catherine,
moreover, allowed sermons to be preached by the Huguenot
ministers in the halls of the palace, and she took care that the
young king would sometimes assist at these instructions.[4]
Her daughter, Margaret of Valois, does not hesitate to write
in her "Memoirs," that the whole court was "infected with
heresy," and that her brother, the Duke of Anjou, "had not
escaped the unhappy influence, for he often used to throw her

[1] The policy pursued by Catherine whilst Queen Regent of France, during the
minority of Charles, is thus faithfully described by Hume:—" She had formed a
plan of administration more subtle than judicious, and balancing the Catholics with
the Huguenots, the Duke of Guise with the Prince of Conde, she endeavoured to
render herself necessary to both, and to establish her own dominion on their con-
strained obedience."—*History of England*, chap. xxxviii.
[2] Capefigue, " Histoire de France," tom. iii., chap. 38 and 41.
[3] Charles IX. hated Spain. In his confidential correspondence with Noailles,
11th May, 1572, we read : " All my thoughts are bent on opposing the grandeur
of Spain, and seeing how I can most dexterously do it."
[4] Letter of the Nunzio *Santa-Croce*, 15th November, 1561, inserted in "Actes
Eccles. civiles et Synodales," tom. i. The famous Calvinist, Duplessis-Mornay,
says of some of his brother ministers that "se fesoient faire la presche en la
chambre de la royne mere du roy pendant son disner, estant aydés à ce faire par
ces femmes de chambre, qui estoient secretement de la religion."—*Cantù*, "Storia
Universale," vol. viii., page 412. "Elle leur donne à entendre qu'elle veut faire
instruire le roi son fils en leur religion."—*Discours Merveilleux*, page xxi.

prayer book into the fire, and give her Huguenot hymns instead."[1] Many French writers are of opinion that Catherine herself "was affected with the venom of Calvinism,"[2] but Mr. White, after a profound investigation as to her character and government, concludes that she had but little of any religion, and that she believed "more in witchcraft and astrology than in GOD."[3] The Spanish ambassador, writing to his court, in 1570, says that in Catherine's royal council of state "five out of the eight members were Atheists or Huguenots."[4] The king himself was weak and vacillating, and wholly intent on the pursuits of pleasure. He was, moreover, impulsive in his anger ; and a writer whom none will accuse of partiality to the Catholic cause, does not hesitate to style him "a furious madman."[5]

Now, however, that the growing influence of Coligny awakened suspicions and alarm in the mind of Catherine, and made her fear lest she would lose her hold of the royal power, she vowed the destruction of the Huguenot leaders. It was rumoured in court-circles that the administration of the government would soon pass into more vigorous hands, and that Coligny would rule supreme as President of the Council and Captain-General of all the forces of the kingdom. "What do you learn in your long conversations with the Admiral Coligny ?" said Catherine one day to the king. "I learn," he hastily replied, "that I have no greater enemy than my mother."[6] These words sealed the doom of Coligny.

Most of the leading Huguenots had hastened to Paris to be present at the marriage festivities of the Prince of Navarre, and they availed themselves of this opportunity to complete their political organization, and to make an imposing display of their numbers and strength in the French capital. The public festivities had not as yet concluded, when Coligny, passing through the streets, received two gun-shot wounds at the hands of an assassin, on the evening of the 22nd of August. The wounds, though dangerous, were not judged mortal. The public voice instinctively traced the attempt to the Queen

[1] " Memoires de Marguerite de Valois," p. 27, *seq.*

[2] " Laboureur," vol. i., page 167.

[3] *White,* " Massacre," page 167. Ranke writes that Catherine " adopted the policy of the Huguenots because she had hopes that by their aid her youngest son, the Duke of Alençon, would mount the throne of England."—(" Hist. de la Papauté," iii., 83.)

[4] "Simanca's Archives."—*Bouille,* ii., page 454.

[5] " History of the United Netherlands," by John Lothrop Motley (London, 1867), vol. i., page 43.

[6] *White,* page 374.

Mother, and authentic history has fully justified that verdict.[1]
In arranging the details of the attempted assassination,
Catherine had for her only assistants her son, the Duke of
Anjou, and the Duchess of Nemours, whose first husband had
been murdered by the Huguenots.

Had Coligny been slain on the 22nd of August, it is probable that no further massacre would have taken place, and
Catherine, without opposition, would have at once resumed
her place at the helm of the State. Now, however, that Coligny
still lived, and that their party was strengthened by the universal sympathy which the attempted assassination had awakened, the Huguenots vowed immediate vengeance against the
assassins. They brandished their swords marching past the
Hotel des Guise,[2] menacing words were even uttered against the
king, and it became their common boast that the broken arm
of Coligny would cost their enemies forty thousand heads.[3]
Above all, angry words were freely used in regard to Catherine.
This artful woman, having failed in this attempt to rid herself
of her defiant rival, saw that not a moment was to be lost to
save herself from utter ruin.

On the morning of the 23rd she hastened to the king, and
unfolded to him the details of a conspiracy[4] which the Huguenots had planned against the State, as well as against himself
and the members of the royal family: one course alone was
open to him to anticipate the traitorous designs of the conspirators, and to turn on themselves the ruin they meditated
against France. "The Huguenots won over the king (thus
writes the acute historian Ranke), and appeared to supplant
Queen Catherine's influence over him. This personal danger
put an end to all delay. With that resistless and magical
power which she possessed over her children, she reawakened
all the slumbering fanaticism of her son. It cost her but one
word to rouse the populace to arms, and that word she spoke.

[1] A number of contemporary authorities will be found in two valuable articles of
the "Revue des Questions Historiques," published by Victor Palmé, Paris, 1866,
livr. 1, page 11, and livr. 2, page 322: also in *White*, page 400, seqq.

[2] *Lavallée* "Histoire des Français," i. page 594: *Dargaud*, "Histoire de la
liberté religieuse," iii., page 255.

[3] Despatch of the Ambassador, *Giovanni Michieli*, in "La Diplomatie Vene-
tienne," page 548.

[4] *Froude* thus describes the discourse of Catherine to the King: "She told him
that at the moment that she was speaking, the Huguenots were arming. Sixteen
thousand of them intended to assemble in the morning, seize the palace, destroy herself, the Duke of Anjou, and the Catholic noblemen, and carry off Charles. The
conspiracy, she said, extended through France. The chiefs of the congregations
were waiting for a signal from Coligny to rise in every province and town."—
"History of England," x. 401.

Every individual Huguenot of note was delivered over to the vengeance of his personal enemy."[1]

Charles, at the request of his mother, signed, without hesitation, a royal mandate for the execution of the Huguenot leaders, and to a chosen band of their enemies was allotted the arduous task of carrying it with secresy into effect. The evening of Saturday, the 23rd, rolled on with all the stillness of a summer vigil in the French capital, and not a murmur foretold the storm that was so soon to burst upon the heads of the unsuspecting Huguenots. But no sooner had the clock of Notre Dame struck three, on the morning of St. Bartholomew's feast, than the bell of St. Germain d'Auxerre tolled the signal for the massacre. The morning's sun of the 24th August saw completed the work of blood, so far as it had been planned by Catherine; but the passions of the populace being once let loose, it was not easy to withdraw them from deeds of violence, and two or three days passed by before order could be fully restored in the capital.[2]

On the evening of the 24th, the King addressed royal letters to the governors of the various cities of France, commanding them to maintain tranquillity, and to preserve the lives of the Huguenots. But the example of Paris proved too contagious for the excited populace, and as soon as the terrible news reached Orleans, Rouen, Lyons, and other towns, fresh scenes of rioting were witnessed, and new names were added to the roll of the murdered Huguenots.

Two days after the fatal festival of St. Bartholomew, the king, by a public order, assumed to himself the whole responsibility of the dreadful massacre; and before the Foreign

---

[1] *Ranke*, "Histoire de la Papauté pendant le 16me siecle," iii. 83.

[2] It is amazing to find with what carelessness the standard Protestant historians deal with the events which they profess to register. Thus, for instance, Hume, in his account of the St. Bartholomew massacre, writes that it began on the evening of the 24th of August : "On the evening of St. Bartholomew, a few days after the marriage, the signal was given for a general massacre of those religionists, and the king himself in person led the way to these assassinations."—("History of England," vol. v., page 147). For this statement regarding the king there is not even a shadow of authority ; and all the contemporary writers are agreed that the massacre took place, not on the evening, but on the morning of the 24th of August. Beza writes that "c'etait au point du jour" ("*Mem. de l'Etat de France*," i. 217). M. Puygaillard, in a letter of the 26th August, 1572, says : "Dimanche matin, le Roi a faict faire une bien grande execution à l'encontre des Huguenotz."—See "Revue des Questions Hist." page 340. To omit other equally explicit statements, the Duke of Anjou attests, that the King and the Queen Mother, with himself and some trusty counsellors, met at the Louvre soon after midnight of the 23rd of August, and at early dawn of the 24th, " ainsi que le jour commençait à poindre," sent a messenger to withdraw the order which had been given for the massacre : but it was too late, the deed was already done.—*White*, " The Massacre," page 416.

Ambassadors and Parliament, assembled in the Gilded Chamber of the Palace of Justice, he made the solemn announcement, that that execution on the leaders of an incorrigible faction which they had witnessed, had been done "by his express orders, not from any religious motive, or in contravention of his edict of pacification, which he still intended to observe, but to prevent the carrying out of a detestable conspiracy, got up by the Admiral and his followers, against the person of the king, the queen-mother, her other sons, and the King of Navarre."[1] Without a dissentient voice, the parliament passed a vote of thanks, commending the King's foresight and energy, and adding its official sanction to the royal sentence already executed against the traitors. To add greater solemnity to the occasion, the whole parliament and court, with Charles at their head, walked in procession to the Cathedral of Notre Dame, and there offered up solemn thanksgiving to God that so great and imminent danger had been averted from the kingdom. Medals were struck to commemorate[2] the event, and it was ordered that the public procession and thanksgiving of parliament should be annually repeated, to perpetuate the memory of their providential escape from the dreadful conspiracy.[3]

It is almost impossible to form an exact estimate of the numbers that were massacred in Paris, and throughout France, on this occasion. Each writer, as impelled by passion or blinded by prejudice, increases the number of the victims, and varies the details of the horrible massacre. Thus, for instance, Perefixe calculates that 6,000 Huguenots were slain in Paris alone, and that the number of the sufferers throughout France was 100,000. Claude Haton writes that more than 7,000 were put to death in the city.[4] Davila and others increase the number to 10,000. Froude[5] states that about two thousand were murdered in Paris, and, "according to the belief of the times," 100,000 men, women, and children throughout France. He adds, however, the significant note, that in this case, as "with all large numbers, when unsupported by exact statistics," it is safe to divide the number "at least by ten." Sully reckons the whole number of victims throughout France

---

[1] The "Official Declaration," in *White*, page 449.
[2] A facsimile of one of these medals is given in vignette of title page by *White* in "Massacre of Saint Bartholomew." It bears the motto, "*Virtus in rebelles*," and serves to confirm the opinion that the Huguenots were punished, not as heretics, but as rebels.
[3] *Saint-Victor*, "Tableau Historique de Paris," xiii., 210.
[4] "Plus de 7,000 personnes bien connues, sans autres jetées dans la riviere, qui ne furent connues."—*White*, page 470. [5] "History of England," x. 408.

as 70,000. Ranke, in his "History of the Papacy," had registered them at about 50,000 ;[1] but in his History of the Wars in
France, he reduces the number to "about 30,000." Hume
estimates the slain in Paris alone as "five hundred gentlemen
and men of condition, and ten thousand of inferior sort." He
does not assign the precise number of the myriads who were
slaughtered elsewhere.

De Thou, writing for the express purpose of promoting in-
fidel Philosophism against the Church, calculates the total
number of the slain in France at 20,000. La Popeliniere, who
flourished at the time, and published his History[2] a few years
after the event, numbers the Parisian victims at one thousand,
and the sufferers throughout the whole kingdom at 20,000.
Papyr Masson reduces the whole number in France to 10,000;
Alzog, to less than 4,000. Caveirac writes that 1,100 were
slain in Paris, and 2,000 throughout the rest of France. Barthelemy adopts the opinion of La Popeliniere as to the city of
Paris, but reduces the total number of the victims throughout
the kingdom to 2,000.[3] Lingard, after a minute examination,
concludes that the total number of the Huguenots slain in all
France did not exceed 1,600. The Huguenot Martyrology[4]
is perhaps the most important contemporary Huguenot record
connected with the St. Bartholomew massacre. It was published in 1582, with the approval of the whole Huguenot body,
who applauded it as an accurate and authentic register of
their martyred brethren. Its authors had access to several
public documents which have since perished, and every local
return which they sought for was readily forwarded by the
various Calvinistic congregations, that thus the work might
be as full and complete as possible. This official Martyrology,
when presenting to the reader a general statement regarding
the massacre, calculates the total number of the victims at
30,000. Subsequently, however, when setting forth the details
for the various districts, the number is reduced to a little more
than 15,000 ; and when, again, it proceeds to calendar the
names of the sufferers, the special purpose for which it was

---

[1] "On a tué pres de cinquante mille."—*Ranke.* " Hist. de la Papauté," etc. iii, 84.
[2] " Histoire de France, depuis l'an 1550 jusqu' en 1577," edit. Paris, 1581, livre,
xxix., p. 66.
[3] The dissertation of M. Ch. Barthelemy, " La Saint-Barthelemy," is one of the
best that has appeared on the subject ; it is found in "Erreurs et Mensonges
historiques," Paris, 1863. The same dissertation is inserted in "Dictionnaire de
controverses historiques," par L. F. Jehan (Migne, 1866), but without the name of
M. Barthelemy.
[4] The following is the full title of this work, to which we will have to recur
more than once : " Histoire des Martyrs persecutès et mis a mort pour la verité
de l'Evangile, depuis le temps des Apôtres jusqu' en 1574," printed in 1582.

composed, it can only discover *seven hundred and eighty-six* victims in the whole kingdom.

Amid so many conflicting opinions regarding the number of the Huguenots who thus fell victims to the perverse policy of the French court, there is one thing at least which we may affirm with confidence, that there is great uncertainty as to the extent of the massacre, and that it is a manifest exaggeration to speak of the St. Bartholomew crime as a general slaughter of all the French Huguenots. When, however, we take into account the perfect organization of the Huguenot congregations throughout France, and when we consider the official weight of the Huguenot Martyrology, and the precision with which it registers in its lists the names even of the humblest sufferers, we cannot be far from the truth when we assert that Lingard, in his computation, has allowed a very wide margin for all possible omissions, and that the total number of the murdered Huguenots cannot have exceeded fifteen hundred.[1] Notwithstanding this massacre of August, 1572, the Huguenots in the following year are found in the field with regularly equipped armies, and fearlessly setting at defiance the whole power of the French monarch. For a while victory even smiled upon them, and when at length they were overpowered by superior strength, the most honourable terms were accorded to them.[2] Their independent organization remained unaltered, and indeed it was not till the time of Richelieu that they at length ceased to form a distinct military power in the kingdom. But it was not the St. Bartholomew massacre, nor their defeat in the field of battle, that effectually broke the power and lessened the numbers of the French Huguenots. For this result France was indebted far

[1] The popular songs of the period point to a very small number of victims. The following, written at the time by Cappler de Vallay, is published by *Cantù* :—

" L'Eternel Diel veritable,
Qui descouvre tous les secretz,
A permis de droit equitable,
Les perfides être massacrez ;
Car la dimanche vingt-quatriesme,
Furent tués plus d'un centieme,
Fauteurs de la loi calvinienne,
Depuis on a continué
De punir les plus vicieux," &c.
 ("Historia Generale," viii. 754).

[2] *White*, page 179, estimates the number of Huguenots in France in 1561 at 1,500,000. After the massacre in 1572 it was calculated that they numbered about 2,000,000.—*Mackintosh*, " History of England," iii., 238. When we take into account that in the intervening period they had been overcome in three civil wars, as we will see hereafter, but little room remains for an extensive massacre of their party on the feast of St. Bartholomew, 1572.

more to the spirit of religion that was awakened throughout the nation by St. Francis de Sales, St. Vincent de Paul, and the clergy formed in their school, whose piety and zeal at length brought back these erring sons into the saving fold of the one true Church of Jesus Christ.

And now, before we quit this portion of our subject, there are a few circumstances connected with the St. Bartholomew massacre which merit our special attention, although they are generally passed over in silence by modern historians.

In the first place, it is an important fact ·that no Bishop or Priest, or other representative of Catholic feelings and Catholic interests, was allowed any part in the Council of Catherine de Medici, and the massacre was planned and devised solely as a matter of State policy. Even the Papal Nunzio was left a stranger to the plot, and, as Sismondi writes, " he only learned the death of Coligny and the rest, when all had been accomplished."

Then, again, several Catholics fell victims to the rage of their enemies on that bloody festival. Sir James Mackintosh expressly asserts that "Catholics were involved in the slaughter: private interests and personal animosities borrowed the poniard and the mask of religious fury."[1] The Huguenot Martyrology[2] cites the following words of Mezeray, an eye witness of the scenes of slaughter: " Whoever possessed wealth, or held an enviable post, or had hungry expectant heirs, was put down as a Huguenot." When recording some individual instances of the massacre, the same Martyrology informs us that the Governor of Bourdeaux caused wealthy Catholics as well as Protestants to be thrown into prison: from Catholics and Protestants alike he demanded a ransom, and he deliberately put to death all for whom the ransom was not paid. Again, it states that at Bourges a Priest was thrown into prison and murdered; that at the town of La Charité, a Catholic matron received the assassin's dagger; and that at Vic the Catholic Governor was himself murdered. It also states that in Paris two Ecclesiastics of high dignity, Bertrand de Villemor and Jean Rouillard, the latter a Canon of Notre-Dame, fell victims in the general massacre. And yet these are only a few cases incidentally mentioned in this record, otherwise so hostile to everything Catholic.

The Protestant historian, La Popeliniere, further assures us that the Catholics of France loudly protested against these deeds of blood being imputed to them, and they readily con-

[1] " History," iii. 225. [2] "Histoire," &c., fol. 731.

tributed as far as was in their power to secure the Huguenots from further attacks : "many more would have been slain," he says, "were it not that some of the Catholic nobility, satisfied with the death of the leaders, used their efforts to appease the mob; several Italians, too, on horseback, and with swords drawn, drove back the rioters in the faubourgs and in the streets, and threw open their houses as a secure refuge for the sufferers ;"[1] he adds the names of several leading Catholics who thus distinguished themselves by sheltering the Huguenots from danger, as the Dukes D'Aumale, de Biron, de Bellievre, &c. The British Museum preserves a curious letter addressed from Paris, in the month of September, 1572, to the English government, which accurately describes the feelings of the Catholics of Paris in regard to the massacre : " it is lamented (it says) to see the King's cruelty, even by the Papists : many be sorry that so monstrous a murder was invented, and at present they dread their own lives. The Duke of Guise himself is not so bloody, neither did he kill any man himself, but saved diverse. He spoke openly that for the Admiral's death he was glad, but that the King had put such to death as, if it had pleased him, might have done good service."[2]

Nor must we suppose that this sympathy of the Catholic citizens for the Huguenots was confined to the capital. In every city of France similar instances were found of that true charity which has ever characterized the Catholic Church, and which, on the present occasion, sought to stem the tide of massacre, and to shield the sufferers by the protecting mantle of religion. Thus, the Huguenot Martyrology, to which we have so often referred, attests[3] that very many of the sufferers were sheltered in the monasteries from the fury of the populace, and as an instance, it states that "the monasteries served as a safe shelter for the Huguenots in Toulouse." Again, it writes that at Bourges "some peaceable Catholics saved the Huguenot sufferers from an infuriated mob." It adds, that in the town of Romans, "sixty

---

[1] *La Popeliniere,* "Histoire," liv. xix.
[2] MSS., Br. Mus.—"News from France," Sept., 1572: *Froude,* "History," x., 410. There is also a Letter of Walsingham, on the 13th of September, in which he writes that "this manner of proceeding is, by the Catholics themselves, utterly condemned." The Venetian Ambassador affirms the same in his "Relazione," published in "La Diplomatie Venitienne :" "Conciossiache dispiaccia oltremodo tanto ai Cattolici quanto agli ugonotti, non dicono tanto il fatto quanto il modo e la maniera del fare; parendo loro di strano che uno la sera si trovi vivo e la mattina morto ; e chiamano questa via e modo di procedere con assoluta potestà, senza via di giudizio, via di tirannide ; attribuendolo alla Regina," &c.
[3] "Histoire," &c. fol. 716.

Huguenots were seized by the mob, but the peaceable Catholics delivered forty of them out of their hands, and the Governor delivered thirteen others. The remaining seven were murdered by private enemies, because they had been found with arms in their hands"—(page 718). At Troyes, a priest was foremost among those who sought to rescue the unfortunate sufferers; whilst at Bourdeaux "several were saved by the clergy and others from whom no such favour could have been expected"—(fol. 730). This triumph of charity over hatred and revenge was nowhere more manifest than at Nismes, notwithstanding the memory of the bitter sufferings to which the Catholics of that city had been a short time before subjected by the triumphant Huguenots. The Catholic citizens, on the first rumours of a massacre, put forth all their strength, and invited the Huguenot leaders to unite with them in order to prevent the shedding of blood. All the city gates were closed except one, and there a body of armed Huguenots were stationed, together with the Catholic troops, to repress every attempt at massacre.

It would not be difficult to multiply proofs of the spirit of charity and forbearance thus shown by the French clergy. The City of Lyons is often cited as an instance of the activity of the priests in the work of slaughter,[1] but Montfalcon, the learned librarian of the public library of Lyons, though writing bitterly against the Catholics, has proved from official documents that the clergy had no part, direct or indirect, in the massacre or other disorders of that city.[2] Fleury attests that the clergy, heedless of what they themselves had so often suffered, used every endeavour to protect the Huguenots:[3] he adds, that the Catholic body in Paris, and throughout all France, openly avowed their disapproval of the massacre. At Lisieux, the Governor, thinking it would please the Court, gave orders that the Huguenots should be put to death, but the illustrious Bishop, John Hennyer, preached with all his zeal against such cruelty, and he not only had the consolation of preserving his flock from the shedding of a single drop of blood, but, moreover, the Huguenots, moved by the charity thus shown them by this good pastor, became docile to his instructions, and very many of them were restored to the fold of Christ.[4] Throughout Burgundy, as De Thou informs us,

[1] As, for instance, by *M. Dargaud*, in his "Histoire de la liberté religieuse," iii., page 362 : notwithstanding its many exaggerations, a prize was awarded to this work by the French Academy.

[2] *Montfalcon*, "Guerres de religion à Lyon," page 420.

[3] "Le clergé, tout maltraité qu'il avait été par les heretiques, en sauva tant qu'il put en differents endroits."—*Fleury*, "Hist. Eccles," 16th century, sect. xii.

[4] *Becchetti*, "Istoria degli ultin i quattro socoli della chiesa," xii., 160.

"little blood was shed, and nearly all the Protestants returned
to the religion of their ancestors."[1] When the Governor of
Dauphiny, Bertrand de Gondes, a devoted Catholic, was told
that it was the King's order that the Huguenots should be put
to death, he replied that "the King's power was abused by
others, and that it was his duty to preserve the King's subjects for him." He, accordingly, issued an order that "any
attempt upon the lives of the Huguenots would be punished
with death."[2] At Dieppe, the Governor assembled the leading
Huguenots in the great hall of the Palace of Justice, and
having announced to them the fate which had fallen on the
rebels in Paris and elsewhere, said he was sure that there
were no rebellious or seditious citizens amongst them, "where-
fore," he added, "children of the same Father, let us live
together as brothers, and having for each other the charity of
the Good Samaritan." No blood was shed in Dieppe, and,
touched by the words of charity addressed to them, many of
the Huguenots vowed to live and die in the Catholic faith.[3]

The question as to whether a royal order was addressed to
the Governors of the various cities and provinces commanding
them to proceed with the punishment of the Huguenots, is
one of but little importance in our present inquiry. There
seems to be but little doubt that some such order was addressed to a few of the Governors, if not by the King himself,
at least by some of the courtiers, in his name. One thing,
however, is now agreed on by friendly as well as by hostile
historians, that no scheme of general massacre had been
arranged by the Court, and communicated to the local
Governors, before the festival of St. Bartholomew. Indeed
it suffices to inspect the dates at which the massacres occurred
in the various districts, to be convinced that they were not
the result of any such preconcerted scheme. At Meaux the
massacre was carried out on the 25th of August; at La
Charité on the 26th; at Orleans on the 27th; at Saumur and
Angers on the 29th; at Lyons on the 30th; at Troyes on
the 2nd of September; at Bourges on the 11th; at Rouen
on the 17th; at Romans on the 20th; at Toulouse on the
25th; at Bourdeaux, not until the 3rd of October. Had the
massacre been executed in accordance with any premeditated scheme, these deeds of blood would undoubtedly have
been perpetrated on the same day throughout France, and the
mere recital of the respective dates must suffice to prove that

---

[1] *De Thou*, tom. vi., page 432 : so also, *La Virotte,* in "Annales d'Arnay,"
1837.
[2] *Long,* "Guerres de Religion dans la Dauphiné :" *Chorier,* "Hist. Dauphiné,"
ii., page 647.　　　　　　　[3] *White,* "Massacre," page 469.

the thirst for blood proceeded from the contagious example of the capital rather than from any orders conveyed to the whole kingdom. Nay, more, in some instances these local massacres were in direct opposition to the express command of the King and Parliament, as at Toulouse, where, some days before the massacre began, "the Parliament published a royal order to the effect that no one should be allowed to molest those of the reformed tenets, but that, on the contrary, every favor should be extended to them."[1]

[1] The " Huguenot Martyrology," fol. 730. It adds that in like manner "the king, by several letters, informed the authorities in Bourdeaux that he did not intend the massacre to proceed further or to extend beyond Paris."

II.

The question will probably have ere this suggested itself: Why were the passions of the Parisian populace so easily excited against the Huguenots, and why, in other towns, were so many people ready, when their hands were loosened, to commit such deeds of bloodshed against these wretched sectaries? Several reasons may be assigned for the bitter feeling thus displayed by the French nation; for us it will suffice to refer to some few of them.

1. In the first place, there was a universal alarm throughout France, lest the Huguenots should seize the helm of Government and enter on the administration of the kingdom. In a neighbouring State, from which they were separated only by the British channel, they had an example of what they might expect under Protestant rule. They heard of the confiscations and imprisonments to which the Catholics of England and Ireland were subjected, the tortures employed to extort confession of guilt from the confessors of the faith, the savage cruelty exercised towards them on the scaffold, and even after death: and they said to one another—Protestantism has triumphed in England, and this is the result: the era of Nero and Diocletian has been revived, and unheard of cruelties have been exercised against the Catholics of that kingdom. Are we to permit the same intolerant spirit of persecution to rule in our Catholic nation? It was not that the Queen-mother or the Court of France felt aggrieved by the persecuting edicts of Queen Elizabeth. A few days after the St. Bartholomew massacre, Catherine addressed a letter to the French Ambassador in London, and when setting forth the reasons of State why the death of Coligny and the other factious leaders should not interrupt the friendly relations that existed between the two powers, she asks: "Did the Court of France manifest displeasure when the Queen of England ordered the death of those who troubled her at home? No; and even were she to order the execution of all the Catholics of England, we would not allow such a matter to interfere with our mutual friendship."[1] Seldom, indeed, are such cynical and heartless words to

[1] "Nous ne vous en empêcherions ni altérerions aucunement l'amitié d'entre elle et nous."—*Correspondance Diplomatique*, tom. vii., p. 347.

be found even in the annals of diplomacy. On another occasion, however, Catherine displayed a little more of the national spirit : for, when Elizabeth instructed the French Ambassador to convey to the King the expression of her hopes that he would be friendly to the Huguenots, the Queen-mother dictated in reply that her royal son could not follow a better guide than his good sister of England, and he would be careful to imitate the example which she would set in her dealings with her Catholic subjects.[1]

The French people felt none of that heartless indifference which ruled at Court. They were fired with indignation at the recital of the atrocities to which their fellow Catholics were subjected in these countries, and it was openly declared that if the Huguenots were allowed to triumph, then the same scenes of butchery would be witnessed among themselves. The feeling in Paris was particularly intense. It is thus described by a modern historian, who, I may remark, is most repulsively prejudiced against everything Catholic: "Honest Catholics, they said, would fare no better in France than they did in England, where, as it was well known, they were every day subjected to fearful tortures. The shop-windows were filled with coloured engravings, representing, in exaggerated fashion, the sufferings of the English Catholics under bloody Elizabeth, or Jezabel as she was called ; and as the gaping burghers stopped to ponder over these works of art, there were ever present, as if by accident, some persons of superior information who would condescendingly explain the various pictures, pointing out with a long stick the phenomena most worthy of notice. These caricatures proving highly successful, and being suppressed by order of the Government, they were repeated upon canvas on a larger scale, in still more conspicuous situations, as if in contempt of the royal authority which sullied itself by compromise with Calvinism."[2]

[1] *Digges*, p. 246 : *Lingard*, vi. 139. In 1567, several of the German Princes, including the Palatine of the Rhine, and the Dukes of Saxony and Wurtemberg, despatched an embassy to the King of France, also interceding in favor of their co-religionists. Charles replied that he would be a friend of theirs only so long as they abstained from meddling in the affairs of his kingdom ; and he added : " I might also pray them to permit the Catholics to worship freely in their own cities." *White*, p. 272. How little changed is the attitude of these German Governments towards their Catholic subjects, even after three hundred years !

[2] *Motley*, " History of the United Netherlands," i. 42. A few years later the same argument was made use of by the French agent who sought to engage Philip the Second in a war against England : " I cannot refrain from placing before your eyes the terrible persecutions which the Catholics are suffering in England ; the blood of the martyrs flowing under so many kinds of torments ; the groans of the prisoners, of the widows and orphans ; the general oppression and servitude, which is the greatest ever endured by a people of God under any tyrant whatever." —*Memorial of Mendoza*, in Motley's " History," i., 129.

2. Another alarming example was at their own doors, in Switzerland, and this came the more closely home to them, because Calvin was in reality the prime-mover of all the Huguenot disorders, and from his mountain retreat in Switzerland was accustomed to boast that, before he died, his Reform would be triumphant in his own native France. Calvinism was indeed triumphant in Switzerland, but it was triumphant, as Erasmus attests, "by the slaughter of more than one hundred thousand, young and old," of the brave Catholic Swiss peasantry.[1] And lest anyone should perchance entertain a doubt as to the tendency of their principles, the French Huguenots, in their Synod held at Paris in 1559, had openly adopted the tenets and discipline of the Swiss Calvinists, and true to the spirit of their founder, they had further enacted the severe statute that "heretics should be punished with death," and that it was "the duty of the State to enforce such punishment."[2] Protestant writers, whilst accusing their Catholic brethren of intolerance, should not be unmindful of these decrees of their Continental co-religionists—decrees the more revolting and intolerable, because they were enacted in the name of liberty, and under the specious pretence of asserting the outraged principles of religious equality.[3]

3. But there was yet another reason why the French populace were so easily roused to vengeance, and as it is one of vital importance for understanding the relative position of parties in France, at the period of which we treat, you will pardon me if I dwell on it at some length.

[1] *Erasmus*, "Opera," tom. iii., part I, p. 900.
[2] See the excellent Dissertation by *Alzog* in *Wetzer and Welte's* "Dictionnaire Encyclopédique," ii. 358.
[3] Beza writes:—" Those who are unwilling to put heretics to death are more guilty than those who allow parricides to live with impunity: we desire to exterminate those who disturb the Church."—(" Profession of Faith," point 5th, p. 119). It was also a saying of Luther that " We live in such peculiar times that a prince may gain heaven more readily by shedding blood than at other times by prayer." When Condé consulted the Calvinist Synod assembled at Orleans about tolerating the Catholic worship, " that impracticable body, while claiming absolute liberty for themselves, would have denied it to those whom they called Atheists, libertines, and anabaptists."—*White*, p. 230. We need not, however, go beyond Great Britain for this teaching of intolerance. John Knox, in his " Appellation," declared that it was the duty of subjects to depose a Catholic queen, " and punish her to death with all the sort of her idolatrous priests." The same intolerance is taught in the Canons of Convocation of 1640; in the solemn League and Covenant; and in Jewell's Apology. And what shall we say of the oath taken by William and Mary as King and Queen of Scotland : " We swear to root out all heretics and enemies to the true worship of God, that shall be convicted by the true Kirk of God of the aforesaid crimes, out of our lands and empire of Scotland." I need say nothing of Protestant teaching and practice in Ireland. No wonder, indeed, that Frederic Seebohm should be obliged to acknowledge, in his history of the " Era of the Protestant Revolution," that " there was one thing especially in which there seemed to be reaction rather than progress during the era, viz., in toleration."—p. 219.

The Huguenots had been labouring for many years, partly by intrigue and partly by force of arms, to overthrow the religion of the nation and to establish the tenets of Calvin in its stead. To attain this great object of their ambition, all means seemed lawful to them. They sought by turns to oppress the Catholics, to revolutionize the State, and to dismember the kingdom. The result was faithfully sketched, a few years later, by the Duke of Burgundy : " I do not now speak," he said, "of the calamities produced by the new doctrines in Germany, England, Scotland, or Ireland : I speak only of France. Nor shall I enumerate one by one the evils of which it was the theatre, which are recorded in so many authentic documents : the secret assemblies ; the leagues formed with foreign enemies ; the attempts against the government ; the seditious threats, open revolts, conspiracies, and bloody wars ; the plundering and sacking of towns ; the deliberate massacres and atrocious sacrileges :—suffice it to say, that from Francis I. to Louis XIV., during seven successive reigns, all these evils, and many others, with more or less violence, desolated the French monarchy. This is a point of history which, although it may be variously related, can neither be denied nor called in question."

4. As early as the reign of Francis I., many of the French courtiers had adopted the reformed tenets. In the religious wars which ravaged Europe in the first half of the sixteenth century, we frequently find the French monarch the ally of the Protestant German States. The purport indeed of such an alliance was a purely political one, to counterbalance the overwhelming influence of Catholic Spain, but it indirectly served to swell the numbers and to increase the authority of the French reformers. Soon after the accession of Charles IX., the Huguenot leaders reckoned themselves sufficiently powerful to attempt to supplant the Duke of Guise and the Catholic party at Court, and under the guidance of Throckmorton, the English Ambassador in Paris, they entered into a plot known as the Conspiracy of Amboise, to seize the helm of State and take the government into their own hands. Owing to the energy of the Duke of Guise, their plans were frustrated. A far more serious attempt, however, was made in 1562, and once more it was the English Ambassador that urged them to draw the sword. Their envoys negotiated a formal treaty with Elizabeth, and English troops, under the command of the Earl of Warwick, landed on the coasts of France, whilst another army of German mercenaries ravaged the fair plains of Normandy. Relying on this powerful aid, the Huguenots rose in arms, and almost on the same day made themselves masters of eighteen

cities and several towns.[1] We will refer just now to some
of the terrible scenes of pillage and bloodshed which ensued;
for the present, suffice it to remark, that the flame of civil war
was kindled throughout all France. The Catholic troops,
however, soon obtained a mastery in the battlefield, several
victories crowned their arms, and the fall of Orleans, the last
stronghold of the Huguenots, was hourly expected, when the
Duke of Guise was treacherously assassinated in the Catholic
camp. The Queen-mother availed herself of this opportunity
to conciliate the contending parties, and conditions of peace,
most favourable to the Huguenots, were accorded by the
crown.

There was one special feature in this Huguenot revolt which
awakened the indignation of the French people. As the
price of English support, the Huguenot leaders had surrendered
Havre and Dieppe into the hands of Queen Elizabeth, and
consented to admit an English garrison into Rouen. Such
treasonable measures indeed excited the displeasure, not only
of France, but of all Catholic Europe, and were hailed with
delight only by the German Lutherans and the Turks. They
failed, however, to secure success for the traitors. Two-thirds
of the English garrison were slain at the capture of Rouen;
Dieppe was almost immediately abandoned as incapable
of defence; and more than half of the Earl of Warwick's
army being wasted by disease and the sword, in the hopeless
defence of Havre, that city, too, after a short siege, was
restored to the crown of France. This unsuccessful attempt
of the Huguenots to recall a hated rival power to the French
coasts, made their revolt doubly offensive to the nation: it was
an outrage, at the same time, against patriotism and against
religion.

5. By the terms of the treaty, sanctioned by the Court, the
Huguenots were allowed the free exercise of their reformed
worship, and no penalty was imposed for their past treasons.
This, however, was far from satisfying the restless ambition
of their leaders. In 1567,[2] they again rose in revolt. "On
the same day (writes Ranke), the insurrection burst forth all
over France. The writers of the period are obliged to go back
to Mithridates, King of Pontus, to find an historical parallel

---

[1] *White*, "Massacre," p. 202, gives the names of several of the cities and districts
thus occupied by the Huguenots.

[2] The Protestant *Sismondi* writes: "A la fin de Septembre 1567, les Huguenots se
rendirent maîtres des villes de Montauban, Castres, Montpellier, Nimes, Viviers,
Saint-Point, Uzès, Pont-Saint-Esprit, et Bagnolles; partout ils chassèrent des
convents et des églises les prêtres, les moines et les religieuses. Ils dépouillèrent
les sanctuaires de leurs ornements, et quelquefois ils démolirent les edifices sacrés."
"Histoire des Français," tom. xviii., p. 10.

for the secresy with which this revolt was organized, and for
the precision and rapidity with which it was carried into effect."[1]
The signal of the war was a treacherous attempt to seize on
the King and the Court in the neighbourhood of Meaux. The
plot, however, was betrayed a moment before its execution,
and the King, with difficulty, escaped to Paris.[2] All France
was again in flames, and once more the English Ambassador,
Norris, is the instigator of the revolt, and the chief support of
the rebels. Queen Elizabeth, indeed, wrote to the King, con-
gratulating him on his providential escape ; but her crafty
minister, Cecil, accompanied her letter by a private despatch
to Norris, instructing him " to comfort the insurgents, and
exhort them to persevere."[3] The Catholic troops, however,
were everywhere victorious ; the government again stepped in
to negotiate terms of pacification, and favourable conditions,
with full liberty of worship, were readily accorded to the
Huguenots. All this only served to convince, more and
more, the Huguenot leaders of the political advantages which
the Government derived from their support, and to increase
their defiant boldness.

6. A third time they rose in arms in 1569. They had now
increased their strength by the aid of German mercenaries,
who were paid with English gold.[4] They were known as
Reiters, and Davila describes them as devastating France
like a frightful hurricane. " Fierce in demeanour, brutal in
habits, as intractable as they were insolent, and a nuisance
alike to friend and foe, they were insatiable pillagers, and their
long train of wagons, filled with plunder, often caused irre-
mediable delay in the march of the Huguenot army."[5] Some
of these had been engaged by the Huguenots in the former
wars, but now they came in increased numbers. Never-

---

[1] Ranke, " Histoire de France," vol. i., p. 259.

[2] The King owed his safety to a select body of Swiss troops, with whom he
marched to Paris. They were attacked on the way by Condé and 500 horse, but
without waiting to give battle they continued their march, " standing fast awhile,
and then retiring, still turning their head as doth the wild boar whom the hunters
pursue."—*La Noue*, p. 395. *White*, p. 277.

[3] See further details in *Lingard*, viii. 61. It was stated at the time, and was
generally believed, that had the Huguenots succeeded they would have burnt Paris.
For proofs, see *J. Cretineau Joly*, " Hist. relig: polit. &c., de la Comp. de Jesus,"
vol ii:, p. 85.

[4] Queen Elizabeth forwarded to Rochelle six pieces of artillery, with their
ammunition. She also sent £50,000 in gold, with a promise of more. She
required, however, a guarantee for repayment, and in the Cotton MSS. (*Caligula*,
E. vi., fol. 90) there is an inventory of jewels and trinkets mortgaged to her by Joan
of Navarre, Condé, and Coligny, on 12th June, 1569.

[5] *White* " Massacre," p. 289.

theless, the decisive battles of Montcontour[1] and Jarnac broke
the power of the Huguenot party, and crushed all their hopes
for the present. They did not, however, cease to conspire,
and though a general edict of pacification was published in
1570, they availed themselves of it only to renew their secret
military organization, and to mature their plans for future
struggles.

7. All this time the Huguenots were but one in ten of the
French population, and the question was asked in every ham-
let and town in France: Is this turbulent faction to be allowed
thus continually to disturb our peace, to seek aid from the
enemies of our nation, to make treaties, and to arm themselves
for our destruction ? Of what use are our victories in the field,
when the jealousy of the Court robs us of their fruit, and each
overthrow of the Huguenots is only the signal for new favours
to be lavished on them by the Queen-mother and the Government ? As a consequence of the prolonged civil wars, the
pursuits of agriculture had been almost entirely abandoned,
and commerce was ruined. In Paris itself " the anarchy seems
to have been complete, each man being a law to himself. Not
even in the terrible revolution that closed the eighteenth
century were the bonds of society more thoroughly relaxed."[2]
A few incidents will best serve to illustrate the state of popular
feeling that prevailed at this time in Paris. On the 27th of
December, 1561, while the Huguenots were attending service
in the church of St. Marcellus, in Paris, the bells of the neighbouring parish church of St. Medard were rung to summon
the Catholics to vespers. This was considered by the Huguenots to be a studied insult, and, accompanied by Beza, 1,500
of their number fully armed, headed by Audelot on horseback,
burst into the church of St. Medard, massacred fifty of the
unoffending congregation, overturned the altar, carried away
the sacred vestments, and trampled under foot the most Holy
Sacrament. The next day the Huguenots assembled again
in St. Marcellus's church, in great numbers, to celebrate their
triumph, but 4,000 citizens, unable to restrain their rage,
attacked the church, dispersed the congregation, tore the pulpit
to pieces, and burned the church to the ground.[3] When the
news of the death of Condé reached the city, after the battle
of Jarnac, in 1569, the Lent-preacher declared it to be a divine

1 The battle of Montcontour, fought on 3rd Oct., 1569, was the most brilliant of
the whole campaign. The Huguenots went into battle 18,000 strong, and before
night it was a difficult matter to collect 1,000 of them to cover their retreat.
—*White*, p. 312.

2 *White*, p. 232.   3 *Becchetti*, " Istoria," x. 338 : *White*, "Massacre," p. 86.

judgment, and described the fallen leader of the Huguenots as "the chief of robbers, murderers, thieves, rebels, and heretics, in France : a prince degenerated from the virtues and religion of his ancestors, a man foresworn, guilty of treason against God and the King, a profaner of temples, a breaker of images, a destroyer of altars, a contemner of the sacraments, a disturber of the peace, a betrayer of his country, and a renegade Frenchman."[1] Again, when the arrangements were being made for the marriage of the King's sister with Henry of Navarre, Joan of Navarre objected to its being celebrated in the capital, on account of the fanatical temper of the inhabitants ; whilst, on the other hand, the Parisians were equally averse to it, fearing, says Claude Haton, "that they would be robbed and despoiled in their houses by the seditious Huguenots."[2] Throughout the marriage festivities the Huguenots were regarded as aliens—"aliens in language, costume, and religion." Both parties "were armed and equipped as if about to enter upon a campaign." The Huguenots looked on the city as a volcano, yet "there were bigots and fanatics among them who seemed to court rather than avoid an explosion."[3]

8. But it is time that I should give some instances of the Satanic cruelty which the Huguenots displayed towards the Catholics, and the vandalism with which they raged against everything held sacred in Catholic faith, wherever a momentary success placed the sword of authority in their hands. In the three wars of 1562, 1567, and 1569, no fewer than fifty cathedrals and five hundred Catholic churches were plundered, the sacred vessels desecrated, the altars destroyed, the paintings and vestments torn to shreds, or applied to profane uses. The principality of Bearn was one of the first to adopt the Genevan tenets, and what was the result? All public acts of Catholic worship were interdicted, the clergy were exiled, and religious toleration was denied to the Catholic subjects. A decree was published in 1571, banishing all superstition and idolatry from the territory, and commanding all to assist at the Calvinist sermons, under penalty of fine or imprisonment.[4] And yet it was in the name of religious liberty that such enactments were made. At Venez, a small town in Languedoc, more than a hundred Catholic prisoners were massacred in cold blood, and their bodies thrown into a well.[5] A plan

---

[1] *White*, p. 306. [2] *Claude Haton* "Memoires," ii., p. 663. [3] *White*, p. 380.
[4] *See* "Declaration pour servir de réglement pour la discipline des églises de Béarn," ap. *Soulier*, "Hist. du Calvinisme," p. 119.
[5] *Memoires* de Jacques Gache, p. 17, seqq.

was organized in Geneva by Calvin, Beza, and others, for the seizure of the city of Lyons, on the 5th September, 1561. The attempt was frustrated by the Catholics, who, however, exercised no violence towards the conspirators. In 1562 the treason of De Sault, the governor, gave possession of the city to the Huguenots. Then the most revolting scenes were witnessed. The destruction of everything sacred was decreed and carried into execution with the greatest violence. "Never did the Goths rage with such fury against the city of Rome as was shown by these sectaries against the desolate city of Lyons;" thus writes de Rubys in his "Histoire veritable de la ville de Lyon," published in 1640. All who refused to fight under the Protestant banner were despoiled of their property, and banished from the city. The life-size silver crucifix in the Cathedral was thrown down by the Huguenot minister, Ruffi, who cried out, "Behold the idol is cast down," and then cut off the head, which he carried to his own house. The silver shrine, in which the body of St. Justus was preserved, was also broken open and carried off: the statues which adorned the façade and portico of the Cathedral were demolished: the tombs were violated in search of treasure: the church of St. Irenæus, and the sanctuary of Notre Dâme de Fourvière were sacked: everywhere the relics of the saints were thrown into the fire, or trampled under foot: and an order was published by the commander, Baron des Adrets, that every citizen, under the severest penalties, should assist at the sermons of the Reformed ministers, "since it is the will of God that idolatry should be banished from amongst us."[1]

This Baron d'Adrets was one of the most active of the Huguenot military leaders. He was, at the same time, pre-eminent among them for his cruelty. "He was, in regard to the Catholics," writes Feller, "what Nero was to the early Christians. He sought out and invented the most novel punishments, which he took pleasure in seeing inflicted on those who fell into his hands. This monster, wishing to make his children as cruel as himself, forced them to bathe in the blood of Catholics whom he had butchered."[2]

At Pamiers, in 1566, as Heylin informs us, the Huguenots fell on the clergy who were engaged in a procession of the Blessed Sacrament, on the festival of Corpus Christi, and massacred them. Similar outrages were witnessed at Mon-

---

[1] "Discours des premiers troubles advenus a Lyon," par *Gabriel de Saconay*, praecenteur et Comte de l'Eglise de Lyon : printed in Lyons in 1569, in 12°. *Revue des Questions Hist.* i. 34.

[2] *Feller*, "Dictionnaire Historique," a. n.

tauban, Rodez, and Valence. In 1562, Languet, who was one of the leading Huguenots, wrote to the Elector of Saxony, that in Gascogne and the Lower Languedoc, as, also, in Provençe, and as far as the Pyrenees, within a range of forty miles, no Catholic priest dared to show himself.[1] At Montpellier, the same year, two hundred Catholics were put to death, the cathedral was pillaged, and Catholic worship was prohibited throughout the district. In 1569, the fanaticism of the Huguenot preachers was pushed to such extremes, that at Orthez three thousand Catholics were butchered; and in the neighbourhood of St. Sever, two hundred priests, who had been arrested in various towns, were cast headlong from a precipice.

9. A few extracts, however, from Mr. White's History[2] of this period, which is derived almost exclusively from Huguenot sources, will best enable us to form an accurate idea of the outrages which were thus perpetrated throughout France, in the name of religion, by the Huguenot disciples of Calvin. Writing of the years 1561 and 1562, he says that the Huguenots "seized upon the churches, drove the monks from their convents, made bonfires of the crosses, images, and relics, and demanded an enlargement of their privileges. During the procession of the Fête Dieu at Lyons, 5th June, 1561, a Huguenot tried to snatch the Host out of the priest's hand. These indiscreet Reformers were the dread of the moderate Beza :[3] 'I fear our friends more than our enemies,' he wrote"—(page 185).

At Tours everything most sacred was outraged: "For some weeks the town was in the hands of the Huguenots, who seized upon the churches, stole the plate, broke the images and ornaments, burnt the service books, desecrated the relics, and ordered every ecclesiastic to leave the place in twenty-four hours, under pain of imprisonment. Contemporary records describe the destruction of a Calvary of gold and azure, one of the wonders of the world, which sixty years before had cost the large sum of ten thousand ducats. The plunder of the churches served to keep up the war. That of St. Martin

---

[1] *Gandy*, "Revue des Questions Historiques," i. 30.

[2] "The Massacre of St. Bartholomew : preceded by a History of the Religious Wars in the Reign of Charles IX.," by *Henry White*. London, 1868. Mr. White, at every page, betrays his feelings of deep hostility against the Catholics, and adopts, most unfairly, the most atrocious tales and accusations against them, on the assertion of their Huguenot enemies. We are, on that account, the more justified in accepting his narrative of the atrocities committed by the Huguenots.

[3] "Nostros potius quam adversarios metuo," 4th Nov., 1561.—*Baum's* "Beza." In another Letter to Calvin, the same Reformer wrote: "you will scarcely believe how intemperate our people are." (18th Jan., 1562).

at Tours furnished Condé (the Huguenot leader) with
1,200,000 livres, without counting the jewels in the shrines.
When the King's authority was restored in Tours, Mass was
ordered to be sung in St. Martin's Church, but everything in
it had been broken or destroyed, except the stalls in the
choir and a few of the painted windows"—(page 216).

At Rouen, "one Sunday in May, the Huguenots, in the
exultation of their triumph, sacked and defaced the cathedral
and thirty-six parish churches. They made such work, says
Beza, 'that they left neither altar nor image, font nor beni-
tier.'[1] That this was not the act of a lawless mob, nor of
a sudden excitement, but of calmness and deliberation, is
probable from what happened about the same time at Caen,
in the same province, where the minister, Cousin, told the
judges that 'this idolatry had been put up with too long, and
that it must be trampled down.' And here the destroyers,
after scattering the ashes of William the Conqueror, breaking
organs, pictures, pulpits, and statues, to the estimated value
of 100,000 crowns, had the impudence to ask the Town
Council to pay them for their two days' work, which was
done"[2]—(page 220.)

In the little town of Montbrison, in August, 1562, under the
command of the notorious Baron des Adrets, "the slaughter
was fearful: more than eight hundred men, women, and
children were murdered ; the streets were strewn with corpses,
and the gutters looked as if it had rained blood," says a
contemporary. All through the south of France, "at the first
outbreak of hostilities, the Huguenots seized upon the churches,
which they purified of all marks of idolatry, destroying the
relics, and making a jest of the consecrated wafer. In some
towns they entirely forbade the Catholic worship." At Lyons,
whilst "liberty of conscience was proclaimed, every convent
was broken open, and the Mass was abolished. The Huguenots committed devastations that would have disgraced
the Vandals. Churches were ravaged, tombs broken open,
coffins stripped of their lead, and their gold and silver plates;
the bells were broken up, and the Basilica of the Maccabees
destroyed by gunpowder"—(page 242).

At La Rochelle, the people, excited "by the violence of the
preachers, rushed to the churches, threw down the altars,
and burnt the images. Some priests who had been shut up

---

[1] Another writer of the time says: " Il a fait piller, ne laissant que les murailles et
que les terres qui ne se pouvaient emporter."—*Canton d'Athis*, p. 44.
[2] This rests on the authority of *De Bras de Bourgeville*, a contemporary.—See
" Memoires de l'Academie de Caen," 1852.

in the lantern tower were stabbed, and thrown half dead into the sea. One Stephen Chamois, a Carmelite monk, had escaped from the city, but being recognised at Aunai, in Saintonge, he was called upon to abjure, and on his refusing to do so, was murdered on the spot '"[1]—(page 242).

At Dieppe (the Rochelle of northern France), the Huguenots are found "pillaging and defacing churches, and melting down the sacred vessels, from which they collected 1,200 pounds of silver. In bands of 200 and 300 they made forays into the adjacent districts, to Eu and Arques, from which they never returned empty-handed. We read of their dragging priests ito Dieppe tied to their horses' tails, and flogging them at beat of drum in the market place. Some were thrown into the sea in their sacerdotal robes ; some were fastened to a cross and dragged through the streets by ropes round their necks; and to crown all, some were buried in the ground up to the shoulders, while the Huguenots, as if playing a game of nine-pins, flung huge wooden balls at their heads. A few weeks after the war broke out, the Protestants of Bayeux rose against the clergy, committing the customary devastations, besides violating the tombs, and throwing out the mouldering corpses. They gutted the bishop's palace, and made a bonfire of the chapter library, then the richest in all France. The priests and others who opposed them were barbarously murdered, and tossed from the walls into the ditch. Once more, in March, 1565, the Huguenots gained the upper hand, when the troops under Coligny refused to be bound by the terms of the capitulation. Private houses were stripped of all the gold, silver, copper, and lead that could be found ; priests who resisted were flogged, dragged up and down the streets by a rope at their necks, and then killed. Children were murdered in their mothers' arms; one Thomas Noel, a lawyer, was hanged at his own window; and an unhappy woman had her face stained with the blood of her own son, who had been killed before her eyes. Here, too, more priests were buried up to the neck, and their heads made to serve as targets for the soldiers' bullets; others were disembowelled, and their bodies filled with straw (that they might burn the better). The priest of St. Ouen—we shudder as we record such horrors—was seized by four soldiers, who roasted him, cut him up, and threw his flesh to the dogs. It would have been well had these deeds of brutality been confined to Normandy, but they were repeated all over France. One Friar Viroleau died of the

---

[1] *Arcere,* " Histoire de la ville de Rochelle," i., p. 358. *Vincent,* " Recherches sur les commencements de Rochelle."

consequences of barbarous mutilation. Other priests or Catholic people were killed by hanging, speared to death, left to die of hunger, sawn in two, or burnt at a slow fire. All this happened in Angouleme. At Montbrun a woman was burnt on her legs and feet with red hot tongs. At Chasseneuil, in the vicinity, a priest, one Louis Fayard, was shot to death after having been tortured, by having his hands plunged in boiling oil, some of which had been poured into his mouth. The vicar of St. Auzanni was mutilated, shut up in a chest, and burnt to death. In the parish of Rivieres others had their tongues cut off, their feet burned, and their eyes torn out; they were hung up by the legs or thrown from the walls"[1]— (page 248).

Towards the close of 1565, the King and Court paid a visit to Joan, Queen of Navarre. She had "swept her dominions of every vestige of Romanism, and denied to her Catholic subjects that religious liberty which she claimed for her co-religionists in France. When returning through the Province of Gascony, Charles, at every step, was reminded of the outrages offered to his religion. As he rode along by the side of the Queen of Navarre, who accompanied him to Blois, he pointed to the ruined monasteries, the broken crosses, the polluted churches; he showed her the mutilated images of the Virgin and the saints, the desecrated grave-yards, the relics scattered to the winds of heaven."—(page 265).

"At Soissons the Huguenots pillaged the churches, demolished the beautiful painted windows, broke the organ, melted the bells, stripped the lead off the roofs, plundered the shrines of their gold and jewels, burned the relics of the saints, and tore up the charters and title deeds belonging to the clergy. Similar tumults occurred at Montauban and other towns"[2] —(page 270).

At Nismes, in particular, the Catholics were repeatedly subjected to persecution. As early as 1562, "the municipal council decided that the cathedral, with some other churches, should be made over to the Reformers, and further ordered the bells of the convents to be cast into cannon, the convents to be let 'for the good of the state,' the relics and their shrines to be sold, and the non-conforming priests to leave the city." It was in 1567, however, on the 30th of September, that the terrible massacre occurred, which is known as the *Michelade*, on account of the pious people of Nismes being

[1] *Vitet*, "Hist. Dieppe," p. 77: *De Bras*, "Antiquites de Caen," p. 170: *Archives Curieuses de France* (Cimber and Danjou), tom. vi., ser. i., p. 299.
[2] *Cimber*, vi., 309: "Discours des troubles," 5th June, 1566.

accustomed to celebrate the festival of St. Michael the Arch-angel on the 29th September, and the two following days. The whole of that terrible day the Catholics of the city were plundered and put to death by a merciless band of Huguenots. The bishop succeeded " in escaping from the mob, who, in their angry disappointment, sacked his palace, and killed the vicar-general. A number of Catholics, including the consul and his brother, had been shut up in the cellars of the episcopal residence. About an hour before midnight they were dragged out, and led into that grey old courtyard, where the imagination can still detect the traces of that cruel massacre. One by one the victims came forth : a few steps, and they fell pierced by sword or pike. Some struggled with their murderers, and tried to escape, but only prolonged their agony. By the dim light of a few torches between seventy and eighty of the principal citizens were butchered in cold blood, and their bodies, some only half dead, were thrown into the well in one corner of the yard, not far from an orange tree, the leaves of which, says local tradition, were ever afterwards marked with the bloodstains of this massacre.[1] In the September of the following year, these brutal scenes of violence were renewed : the city was again plundered, and its streets were dyed with Catholic blood. The governor was shot and thrown out of the window, and his corpse was torn in pieces by the lawless mob. In the country round Nismes, forty-eight unresisting Catholics were murdered ; and at Alais, in the neighbourhood, the Huguenots massacred seven canons, two grey friars, and several other churchmen...Even the dead were not left in peace : in more than one instance the corpses were exhumed and treated with savage barbarity."[2]—(page 285).

In 1568 and 1569, the Huguenots, "in their fury, once more defiled the altars, destroyed the churches, and perpetrated a thousand atrocities. Briquemaut, one of their leaders, cheered them on to murder, wearing a string of priests' ears

---

[1] " Le vicaire général, Jean Peberan. est livré aux insultes de la populace, trainé avec une grosse corde et précipité dans le puits ; il avait voulu mourir à la place de l'évêque. Le massacre avait commencé à onze heures du soir ; il dura toute la nuit et continua le lendemain. Ce jour-la, toutes les maisons des Catholiques sont recherchées ; ceux qu'on arrete sont égorgès et jetés au puits. Bien qu'il ait plus de sept toises de profondeur et quatre pieds de diametre, il est presque comblé de cadavres ; l'eau, mêlée de sang, y surnage ; des gemissements étouffés s'en exhalent ; cent cinquante, suivant les uns, trois cents, suivant les autres, furent égorgés." —*Revue des Quest. Hist.* i. 45.

[2] *Barugnon,* " Histoire des Nimes," tom. ii. See also *Vaissette* " Histoire Gen. de Languedoc," v. p. 298 ; and *Menard*, " Histoire de la ville de Nismes," tom. v. p. 16. This last named writer states that most of the authorities in Nismes were secretly favourable to the Huguenots, and hence permitted them to rage with impunity against the Catholics.

round his neck.[1] When the town of Orthez was stormed, so
many of the inhabitants were put to death, without distinction
of age or sex, that the river Gave was dammed up by the
number of bodies thrown into it.   The monasteries and nun-
neries were burnt, not one inmate escaping, the total slaughter
being estimated at three thousand. When the citadel was
taken, every ecclesiastic who was proved to have borne arms,
and the proof was none of the strictest, was bound hand and
foot, and tossed over the bridge into th : river. At Aurillac
they buried some Catholics alive up to the chin, and after a
series of filthy outrages, used their heads as targets for their
muskets. Four hundred persons were put to death there, of
whom one hundred and thirty were heads of families"[2]
—(page 295).

This recital of atrocities will, I am sure, suffice to explain
how it was that the French populace, especially in the districts
which were the theatres of such crimes, were so ready to
engage in deeds of retaliation, and it will also prove that it
was the aim of the Huguenots to exterminate if possible the
Catholics of France. The Huguenot blood, shed on the feast
of St. Bartholomew, 1572, was only as a drop in the ocean
when compared with the torrents of the blood of Catholics
shed by their relentless enemies in almost every city of France.

[1] This fact of Briquemaut wearing a necklace of the ears of the priests whom he
had massacred, is mentioned by all the contemporary writers. The same savage
ornament was also worn by another Huguenot in 1562, but his name is not given.
—*White*, p. 248.

[2] *De Thou*, vol. v., p. 610.

III.

It now only remains to make some comments on a few of the many questions which have arisen in connection with the St. Bartholomew Massacre.

1. And first of all it will be asked what sympathy was shown by the government of England to their Huguenot friends in the terrible disaster which had thus befallen them ? England, during the preceding years, had entered into secret treaties with the Huguenots, and they were publicly regarded as her allies. We would, therefore, expect that she would now avenge the St. Bartholomew outrage, or at least resent, as done to herself, the injury and insult offered to the Huguenot cause. Nothing, however, of all this occurred. A few days after the Massacre the King of France commissioned his ambassador in London, La Motte Fenelon, to explain to Queen Elizabeth the peculiar circumstances of the sad event, and in obedience to these instructions he set before her Majesty that his Sovereign, quite against the royal wishes, had been compelled to act with severity against Coligny and his adherents, on account of a wicked plot they had entered into against the throne, and that if some few innocent persons had suffered with the guilty, this was owing to circumstances which his Majesty was unable to control, and which occasioned him the most heartfelt grief. Elizabeth received the ambassador at Woodstock. The court chronicler records that she was arrayed in the deepest mourning, and that all the lords and ladies who attended her were dressed in black. The whole sympathy, however, of England for the unfortunate dupes of her deceitful policy ended here. Amicable relations were almost immediately re-established, and the friendship of the two courts seemed more closely cemented than ever in the blood of the Huguenots. The English

C

ambassador was instructed to proceed with the negotiations for the marriage of Queen Elizabeth with the Duke d'Alençon, brother of Charles IX., as if nothing had occurred to mar the harmony between their respective courts; and when, a few months later, a daughter was born to the French King, Elizabeth consented to become godmother to the infant princess. She sent the Earl of Worcester on this occasion to present a font of gold as a baptismal gift, and to assist at the ceremony of baptism in her name.[1]

So completely, indeed, did Queen Elizabeth and the English government seem to have overlooked the St. Bartholomew outrage, that the Huguenots regarded their proceedings ·as a studied insult offered to themselves. They pushed their resentment so far as to attack the English ambassador whilst sailing from England to France. One of the ships in his suite was taken and plundered, some of his attendants were slain, and he himself was, for a time, in jeopardy of his life. A little later the Marshal de Retz was sent as a special envoy from Charles to the English court, and the report was generally credited at the time that he received an express acknowledgment from the Queen that Coligny and his associates had deserved their fate.

2. And now a few words as to the question which was warmly debated in former times, whether the St. Bartholomew massacre formed part of a long premeditated scheme of the French court, or was merely prompted by the difficulties which, in consequence of the failure of the attempt on the life of Coligny, had suddenly beset Catherine de Medici and her friends. There are some, indeed, who go so far as to affirm that the plan for the extirpation of the Huguenots was long before arranged by the King and his council; that the honours and caresses shown to Coligny, and even the marriage of the princess Marguerite, formed part of the scheme, the better to lull the suspicions of the intended victims, and to attract them to the capital. This opinion, however, rests on no historical grounds. Everything leads to the conclusion that Coligny had acquired a real mastery over the affections of Charles IX., and it is preposterous to suppose that that young monarch, so weak, and vacillating, and impulsive, could have been such a master of dissimulation as to deceive Walsingham and the other foreign ambassadors, as

[1] *Camden*, page 275 : *De Thou*, iii. 244 : *Castlenau*, tom. xlvi. 55 : *Lingard*, vi. 142.

well as his own courtiers, into the belief that he was favourable to the Huguenots, whilst in reality he meditated their destruction. There perhaps is somewhat more of probability in the opinion that Catherine de Medici had, for some months at least, planned in her own mind this plot for cutting off the leaders of the Huguenots, and possibly she had not forgotten the remarkable advice given to her by the Duke of Alva, who, at the conference of Bayonne, in 1565, as Henry of Navarre attests, put Tarquin's gesture into words, and counselled Catherine to rid herself of the obnoxious noblemen by the curious Spanish proverb that "one salmon's head is better than a hundred frogs."[1] Catherine, however, was not a person to readily suppose that the Spanish statesman was disinterested in his counsel, and that his advice was solely given her in the interests of France. Whether or not, however, the Spanish proverb may have lingered in her mind, it is now generally supposed that, if any such plot existed, the Catholic leaders were likely to share in the fate of the Huguenots, and that had she been successful in the first attempt on the life of Coligny, the Duke of Guise would have been her next victim. But now, that that attempt had failed, she needed the strong arm of this brave nobleman to sustain the government against the Huguenots, and to this circumstance alone he owed his safety. Be this as it may, Catherine, a few days after the massacre, avowed that she had given orders for the death only of a half dozen of the Huguenot leaders, and that "she was responsible in conscience only for that number."[2]

For us this is not a question of great moment, and we will readily leave it to be settled by the friends and admirers of Catherine de Medici, and of the court of Charles IX. Whether the massacre was premeditated or not, it is manifest from the line of policy pursued by Catherine, and from the principles which guided the French court, that the Catholic Church and the Holy See had no part in it, and are in no way responsible for its terrible excesses. Paris witnessed other bloody scenes in 1792 and 1793. Religion was not responsible for them. They were decreed by an Atheistic policy in the name of the sovereign people. The St. Bartholomew massacre was the result of an equally irreligious intrigue, although it was,[3] nominally at least, carried into exe-

---

[1] *Davila*, lib. 3 : *Mathieu*, "Hist. de France," i. 283 : *White*, page 262.
[2] *Ranke*, "Hist. de la Papaute," iii. 83.
[3] "The Massacre of St. Bartholomew, in 1572, was the diabolical work of the queen, Catherine de Medici, to maintain her political power."—*Seebohm*, "The Era of the Protestant Revolution" (Longmans, 1874), page 211.

cution in the interests of the crown. It was the age of classic studies, and it is possible that amid the peculiar difficulties which now beset her, Catherine may have recalled to mind the massacre so famous in Roman literature, when Scylla sought by one blow to rid himself of all his enemies, and, at his command, the streets of Rome on one day flowed with the blood of 6,000 citizens. But whether or not this vision flitted before the mind of Catherine, it is unquestionable that the Catholic Church had as little part in the Parisian crime as in that of Scylla ; and an eloquent writer has well remarked, that were a Blanche of Castile, or a St. Louis on the throne of France in 1572, such a massacre would have been impossible.

3. The important question now presents itself: How was the intelligence of the St. Bartholomew massacre received in Rome? The news, as conveyed to the eternal city, was to the effect that a widespread conspiracy of the Huguenots had been discovered only a moment before their plans were matured, that their wicked designs had recoiled upon their own heads, and that the Huguenot power was now for ever broken in France. This intelligence was hailed with the greatest delight. The city bells rang out their merriest peals, a royal salute was given from the cannon of St. Angelo's, the Pontiff, with the court and clergy, walked in procession from the Basilica of San Marco to the French Church of St. Louis, and the *Te Deum* was solemnly chanted in thanksgiving. In addition to all this, a gold medal was struck to commemorate the happy event, and the whole scene, by command of Pope Gregory the Thirteenth, was represented among the fresco decorations with which Vassari was then adorning the Sala Regia in the Vatican. All this, however, does not prove what the enemies of the Holy See contend, that the Sovereign Pontiff, or the citizens of Rome, gave expression to their joy for a cold-blooded massacre of the French Huguenots.

To fully appreciate the course pursued by the Roman court, we must bear in mind the official intelligence relative to the massacre, which was conveyed by Charles IX. to His Holiness. A special agent was sent to Rome, and his instructions were in substance a mere repetition of the King's discourse in parliament on the 26th August, setting forth the conspiracy of Coligny and his associates, and how their wicked attempt had recoiled on their own heads. The French agent also brought with him a letter to the Pope from Louis de Bourbon, Duke of Montpensier, which attested that the Huguenots had conspired against the life of the King, the Queen mother, the King's brothers, and all the princes and Catholic gentlemen

of their suite, "to the end that Coligny might create a king of
his own religion, and abolish every other religion in the
kingdom: that, providentially, the conspiracy was discovered,
and on the day they had designed to carry out their enterprise,
execution fell upon them and their accomplices, so that all the
chiefs of the sect, and several of their party, were slain."[1]
The Nunzio, Salviati, sent at the same time a full account of
the massacre, and transmitted with it the substance of the
King's discourse in parliament: "that his Majesty, thanks
to Christ, detected a plot which Admiral Gaspar de Coligny
had prepared against the royal authority, so that a terrible
destruction and death threatened the whole family of the
King ; and, therefore, he inflicted on the Admiral and his
followers the punishment which they deserved."[2]

Indeed this account was persistently repeated by the French
envoys at every court, and those who wished to maintain
friendly relations with France were of necessity obliged to
accept it as an official statement of the facts and circumstances
of the case. The Duke of Alva was at this time carrying
on the siege of Mons, in the Netherlands : when he received
the official despatch from Paris, he at once embodied it
in a circular to all the governors of the Provinces, declaring
that "the Huguenots had resolved to murder the King
and the royal family, and to seize on the government:
that for this purpose Coligny had organized a body of 4,000
men in the faubourg St. Germain, but, the secret being betrayed, the King had anticipated their wicked designs, and
thus secured the peace of the kingdom. Four hours later the
storm would have fallen upon the King and the leaders of the
Catholics of France."[3] The French Ambassador in Switzerland, M. de Bellievre, was also commissioned to lay before
the Swiss Diet, then assembled in Baden, the motives which
prompted him to such severity against the Huguenots. His
discourse on the occasion is still extant. He declares that
the execution ordered by the King was an act of justice,
rendered imperative by the conduct of Coligny and his associates. "They had formed a plot, he said, to introduce a
dangerous tyranny into the kingdom. His Majesty, therefore,
seeing the imminent danger to which his crown and life were
exposed, took the advice of the princes and officers of state,

[1] This letter is published from the Vatican Archives, in continuation of the
Annals of Baronius, by *Theiner*, vol. i., page 336.
[2] *Theiner*, i. 45.
[3] This document was discovered in 1842, in the State Archives of Mons, and
was read by M. Gachard for the Academy of Sciences, in Brussels, on the 4th of
June, 1842.

and with their counsel proceeded to exercise strict justice against the leading conspirators."[1]

We are not, however, without direct proof that the motive of the rejoicings in the eternal city was the providential discovery and extinction of a dangerous conspiracy which aimed at the lives and liberties of the Catholics of France. Soon after the news of the massacre had reached Rome, the famous latinist, Muretus, was selected to deliver the usual sermon at one of the thanksgiving ceremonies, in presence of the Pope and the Papal court, and his discourse has happily been preserved. A few of its sentences will suffice to set before us in its true light the whole matter of this solemn thanksgiving : " The Huguenots (he says) did not hesitate to conspire against the life and liberty of that King, from whom, notwithstanding their atrocious deeds, they had received not only pardon, but kindness and affection. In which conspiracy, at the very time that they had marked out and decreed for carrying into effect their wicked design, the destruction which they had plotted against the King, and against almost all of the royal house and family, was turned upon the heads of the wicked traitors themselves. Oh! memorable the night which, by the execution of a few seditious men, thus freed the sovereign from imminent danger of murder, and the whole kingdom from the incessant alarms of civil war."[2]

With these words before us, the whole course pursued by the Sovereign Pontiff and the Roman people becomes clear and intelligible. Were the deluded conspirators Catholics instead of Huguenots, the same thanksgiving would have been offered up, that God had vouchsafed to strengthen the Most Christian King, and to avert so great a calamity from his devoted Catholic nation. The Abbate di San Salvatore was at this time in Rome, as agent of Emanuel Filibert, Duke of Savoy. He writes to the Duke on the 5th of September,

[1] MSS. National. St. Germain, 1247.

[2] "Veriti non sunt adversus illius regis caput ac salutem conjurare, a quo, post tot atrocia facinora, non modo veniam consecuti erant, sed etiam benigne et amanter excepti. Qua conjuratione sub id ipsum tempus, quod patrando sceleri dicatum ac constitutum est, in illorum sceleratorum ac foedifragorum capita id quod ipsi in regem et in totam prope domum ac stirpem regiam machinabantur. O noctem illam memorabilem, quae paucorum seditiosorum interitu regem a praesenti caedis periculo, regnum a perpetua civilium bellorum formidine liberavit... O diem denique illum plenum laetitiae et hilaritatis, quo tu, Beatissime Pater, hoc ad te nuncio allato, Deo immortali et divo Ludovico regi, cujus haec in ipso pervigilio evenerant, gratias acturus, indictas a te supplicationes pedestris obiisti. Quis optabilior ad te nuncius adferri poterat? aut nos ipsi quod felicius optare poteramus principium Pontificatus tui, quam ut primis illius mensibus tetram caliginem, quasi exorto sole, discussam cerneremus." (Opera MURETI, tom. i., page 197, edit. Ruhnken).

1572, informing him that the official news of the massacre had that day reached Rome, and was received with unbounded delight by all, "on account of the interests of the King of France, and of the kingdom and the Church being at stake." He adds, however, and his words abundantly prove that the rejoicings in the eternal city were not the result of frenzy or savage exultation at the wilful shedding of innocent blood; that "far greater would have been the satisfaction of every-one if his Majesty could, with safety, have attained his purpose without dispensing with the formalities of law. Nevertheless, everyone returns thanks to God, being persuaded of the just intentions of his Majesty."[1]

It would be easy to add other testimonies to prove that such was, indeed, the opinion prevalent in Rome, and such the motive of the rejoicings and thanksgiving of the Papal court. Early in the following century the celebrated. Strada composed, in Rome, his History of the War in Flanders. Treating of the St. Bartholomew massacre, he styles it "a signal deed and a punishment deservedly incurred by a faction of conspirators against their sovereign."[2] Pagi, in his Life of Gregory XIII., also writes that that Pontiff viewed the massacre as a necessary act of self-defence of the French court, and, therefore, ordered the thanksgiving : "*actis publice Deo gratiis de periculo a Colinii conjuratione evitato.*"[3]

There were not wanting, indeed, some special reasons why Rome should not regret that a just retribution had fallen on Coligny and his associates. It had been for centuries the anxious care of the Roman Pontiffs to combine the sovereigns of Europe in a holy league to check the advance of the Moslem armies. The leaders of the so-called Reformation pursued a different course. Luther even went so far as to avow his desire to enter into league with the Turks against the Catholic powers, that thus he might in some way weaken the influence of Rome, and he publicly preached that to fight against the Turks was to war against God.[4] True to this evil policy of the Reformers, Coligny presented to the King, in 1572, a memorial to dissuade him from attending to the counsels of Rome, and urging him to marshal his armies

---

[1] *Archivio Storico Italiano*, appendix, tom. iii., page 169.

[2] " Insigne facinus sed meritum conjuratae in regem factioni supplicium.—*Strada*, " De Bello Belgico," lib. vii. page 250.

[3] Brev. Gest. Rom. Pontif. vi. 729.

[4] Among the propositions which Luther refused to retract at the Diet of Worms, 1521, was the following, viz. : " Proeliari adversus Turcas est repugnare Deo." *Opera Lutheri*, tom. ii., page 3 : *Audin*, " Life of Luther," page 174.

against Spain rather than against the Turks.[1] The Huguenot
leaders were also known to be in secret league with the ban-
ditti who at this time infested the several states of Italy. So
numerous were these bands of freebooters, that their united
strength was supposed to be a match for an army of 30,000
men. Their attacks were principally directed against the
States of the Church, and their ravages often filled the citizens
of Rome with alarm. By the destruction which now fell upon
the Huguenots, the Italian bandits lost their chief support,
and being deprived of their war material and other resources,
the field soon became clear for their final overthrow.

Notwithstanding these various motives, the Sovereign Pontiff, Gregory XIII., when freely treating of the occurrence
with his private friends, was far from approving of the St.
Bartholomew massacre : he even burst into tears, and said to
those around him : "Alas! how can I be sure that some innocent souls may not have suffered with the guilty?" Maffei,
the annalist of this Pontiff's reign, having stated that Coligny's
death was announced to His Holiness, as "ordered by the
King, in defence of his own life and kingdom,"[2] further assures
that although Rome was thus freed from a sworn enemy, yet
"the Pope showed a tempered joy, as when a diseased limb is
cut off with pain from the body."[3] Brantome's testimony is
equally conclusive; he thus writes: "touching the joy and
content the good and holy Pope showed concerning the massacre, I heard from a man of honour who was then in Rome,
and who knew the matter well, that when the news was
brought him he shed tears, not for joy, as men ordinarily do
in such cases, but through grief : and when some of those who
were present remonstrated that he should weep and be sad
on the news of the goodly execution of wicked men, enemies
of God and of His Holiness, 'Ah!' he said, 'I weep at the
course which the King has pursued, illegal and forbidden by
God, to inflict punishment in such a manner, and I fear lest
the like shall fall, and that before long, upon himself. I also
weep because, among so many victims, as many innocent as
guilty may have fallen.'"[4]

Twelve days after the news of the massacre had reached the

---

[1] *De Thou*, tom. vi., page 34. The Calvinists continued for a long time to
pursue the same policy. Even under Louis XIV. their great preacher, Jurieu,
declared that the Turks had received a divine mission to co-operate with the
Reformers in the great work of the Gospel: "pour travailler avec les Reformés
au grand œuvre de Dieu."
[2] "Per sicurezza della sua persona e quiete del regno."
[3] *Maffei*, "Annali," lib. i., sec. 20.
[4] *Brantome*, "Memoires de l'Amiral de Chatillon," tom. viii., p. 176.

Vatican, a partial Jubilee, with its special devotions and indulgences, was celebrated in the eternal city. Lord Acton, and the enemies of the Holy See, assure us that this Jubilee was granted by the Pope that the faithful might return thanks to God "for the murder of the Huguenots," and implore courage and strength for Charles IX. to complete his good work "by exterminating all the heretics that yet remained in the kingdom."[1] You will deem it unnecessary for me to remark that no such motives were assigned by His Holiness for this Jubilee, and, indeed, no contemporary document, or other ancient record, has dared to impute such motives to the Pontiff. The whole statement rests on an artful interpretation of a passage in the Jubilee Bull, which invites the faithful "to return thanks for the happy victory of the King of France over his Huguenot enemies, and to pray that these most noxious heresies may be entirely banished from that kingdom, once so renowned for its religion and piety."[2] It needs no great acumen to understand how great a difference there exists between "extirpating the heretics" and "banishing heresy" from a Catholic kingdom : the latter alone, and not the former, was commended to the prayers of the Roman citizens. It is fortunate, however, in the interests of historic truth, that one authentic document has come down to us connected with this Jubilee, which of itself suffices to remove all doubts as to the purposes for which it was granted. This is the contemporary Diary of Francesco Mucanzio, Pontifical Master of Ceremonies,[3] who registered, day by day, the religious ceremonies as they were celebrated in Rome in 1572. He informs us that on the 17th September, in that year, the Jubilee began, which was ordered by His Holiness "for the conversion of heretics, the success of the Christian armies against the Turks, and the election of a king for Poland."[4] Thus it was not to rejoice in the murder of the Huguenots that the Jubilee was celebrated, but to promote three great religious purposes, dear to the heart of Pope Gregory XIII. The Turks, notwithstanding the overthrow at Lepanto, were

[1] Lord Acton's Letters to the *Times*, November, 1874.

[2] " Ad regnum antea religiosissimum a pestilentissimis haeresibus omnino expurgandum."

[3] " Diaria Francisci Mucantii Caeremoniarum magistri." MS. preserved in the Archives of the Gesù, Rome.

[4] See " Revue des Questions Hist." 2de livrais, p. 381. The Papal Medal, which was struck on this occasion, bears the inscription, " In perduellos iterumque nova molientes haereticos."—*Bonanni*, " Numismata Pontificia," i., 336. Thus it was not the murder of the Heretics that was commemorated, but the triumph of the King over his rebel subjects. *Capefigue* mentions another medal struck at this time in France, with the French motto : " Charles IX. dompteur des rebelles," chap. 44.

at that moment menacing a new invasion of Europe; whilst the election of a King of Poland was to take place in a few weeks, and from it, too, depended, in a manner, the fate of all Catholic Europe: no wonder, indeed, that the Pope should ask the faithful to redouble their fervent prayers in such a crisis of society as of the Church. Moreover, it was hoped that as the Huguenots relied on the arm of the flesh for their religious tenets, their conversion might result from their recent humiliation, and, therefore, His Holiness makes this, too, one of the great intentions of the Jubilee, and urges the citizens to offer their prayers that God would look down in mercy upon France, and restore its straying sons to the one true fold.

From all this it must be sufficiently manifest that it is a vile calumny against the Roman Pontiffs to assert that the Papal court and the people of Rome rejoiced at the cold-blooded assassination of the French Huguenots.

4. There is one other matter which merits our attention before we close: it is the principle which guided the conduct, and subsequently became the plea of justification, of the French monarch, Charles IX. This was none other than the principle of assassination legalized by the command of the sovereign. At the present day, as in the ages of Faith, the bare mention of such a principle suffices to excite a thrill of horror, but it was far otherwise in the first century of the Reformed creed, when the influence of religion was weakened, and passion and frenzy obtained full mastery over men's minds.

It is not too much to say, that that foul principle of assassination had become a recognised rule of the degenerate diplomacy and corrupt court life of the period of which we treat, a principle, moreover, of which the Huguenots of France and the Protestants of England had but little reason to complain. Indeed, as well in theory as in practice, it was adopted by the Huguenots themselves, and throughout all Europe none were found to reject the assassin's ministry save those who, not merely in fancy and in name, but in reality and in truth, were loyal children of the Catholic Church. But before I enter on this subject I wish to cite for you the words of Baron Hubner, who, in our own days, has been distinguished alike as historian and diplomatist. In his " Life of Sixtus the Fifth" he thus writes: " What would now-a-days be said of a government which would allow a man's life to be taken without having him previously tried? It would be universally condemned, or rather such a contingency is no longer possible. It was not always so. Even in the time of the Guises, the Sovereign was looked upon as the supreme judge, who, it is true, had bequeathed his rights to competent tribunals, but who could dispense with their aid whenever the public safety, or that of his own person, seemed to require it."[1]

When the Duke of Guise, the leader of the French Catholics, had taken the city of Rouen, in 1562, a Huguenot gentleman attempted to stab him with a poignard, but was taken in the act. In excuse he pleaded that he made this attempt, not through any personal spite, but solely in the interests of his religion. "Well," replied the Duke, "I will show you that my religion is more generous than yours. You say that your religion bids you kill me, who have done you no harm ; now mine commands me to pardon you, who have sought my life:" and so saying, he set him at liberty. Two months later this great Catholic leader was assassinated by another Huguenot, named Poltrot, who, before execution, avowed that he was employed to perpetrate this deed of blood by the Admiral Coligny,[2] and that the Calvinist preacher, Beza, had commended and encouraged him in its execution. Sismondi is forced to admit this fact, but he seeks to exculpate the great Calvinist Reformer by the principles and maxims of the age.[3]

The next Duke of Guise, who also was the life and soul of the Catholic party, met his death in like manner at the hands of an assassin. We have seen that in the terrible deeds of the St. Bartholomew massacre, the Duke of Anjou, brother of the King, took a leading part. He subsequently mounted the French throne as Henry the Third, and jealous of the popularity of the Duke of Guise, and the success which everywhere attended his arms, caused him to be assassinated, together with his brother the Cardinal de Guise. He even wrote to his ambassador in Rome to justify the horrid deed,

---

[1] *Hubner*, "Sixtus the Fifth," i. 22. English edition. London, 1872.

[2] *Trognon*, though an admirer of Coligny, writes that "la haute raison de Coligny était à ce point troublée par le fanatisme, qu'elle ne désavouait point la doctrine perverse du tyrannicide." "Histoire de France," tom. 3, p. 280. *Martin* makes a somewhat similar apology for Coligny : "Coligny n'avait pas suggéré le fait consommé, mais il croyait à la légitimité du tyrannicide inspiré par le ciel." "Histoire de France," ix. 154. *Lavallee*, however, writes: "Coligny laissa comprendre qu'il connaissait les menaces de Poltrot, qu'il l'avait mis à même de les accomplir et qu'il n'en ressentait pas d'horreur." "Histoire des Français," i., 570. *Revue des Questions Hist.*, i., 35.

[3] *White*, "Massacre," p. 228, contends that the statement of Poltrot in regard to Coligny was made in the hope of pardon, but admits "that Coligny assented, if he did not consent, to the crime." He adds : "This may diminish the lofty moral pedestal on which some writers have placed the Protestant hero ; but he was a man, and had all a man's failings.... The murder was openly defended (by the Huguenots), Poltrot was compared to Judith, and ballads were sung in his praise." The "Histoire de l'Eglise Gallicane." liv. xix., p. 956, proves that Poltrot was the agent of the whole Huguenot body.

declaring that it was "not only lawful but pious, seeing that it had for its object to insure the peace of the public by the death of a private individual."—(Letter of Henry to the French Ambassador, Pisany, December 24th, 1588). Seven months later, Henry the Third was himself assassinated, and Henry of Navarre, the hope of the Huguenots, became sovereign of France.

Neither can it be said that the English reformed courtiers were strangers to the use of the secret dagger and to the principle of assassination. When the youthful Reginald Poole, having completed his studies on the Continent, paid his first visit to his near kinsman Henry VIII., and when the hum of flattery was heard around him on every side, and the highest dignities of the Church of England were marked out as already within his reach, Thomas Cromwell, taking him aside, presented to him a copy of the *Prince* of Macchiavelli, telling him that that precious work should be his guide and text-book if he aspired to be a true servant of his royal master.[1] Happy for Poole that he chose higher and nobler principles, but yet Cromwell had stated the truth, for Macchiavelli's teaching was adopted as the rule of the English Court, and marked out the only high road to honours and emoluments in Church and State. I need not add that the principle of assassination, when judged expedient by the royal authority, is broadly and openly justified in the pages of the unprincipled Florentine. Let us see, however, how his teaching was put into practice by the courtiers of Elizabeth at the period of which we treat.

A few days after the St. Bartholomew massacre, the English Ambassador, Walsingham, wrote to Queen Elizabeth, suggesting that Mary Queen of Scots, now a prisoner in her hands, should be privately assassinated—"certain unsound members," he says, "must be cut off, for violent diseases will have violent remedies." The Bishop of London, Edwin Sandys, added his prayer to Burleigh in the same strain: "furthwith to cutte off the Scottish quene's heade: ipsa est nostri fundi calamitas."[2] Nor did her Majesty lend an unwilling ear to these suggestions. She, without delay, sent her trusty agent Killigrew into Scotland, ostensibly to compose some differences that had arisen between the Regent and the Earl of Huntley, but in reality, as the State Papers have placed beyond the reach of doubt, to make arrangements with the reformed

---

[1] This fact is mentioned by Cardinal Quirini in the preface to his noble edition of the letters of Cardinal Poole.

[2] *Ellis*, "Original Letters," 2nd series, iii. 25.

leaders in Scotland for the assassination of her august prisoner, Mary Stuart.[1]

The same principle held a prominent place in the policy of Elizabeth in regard to Ireland, and every student of our history is now familiar with the repeated efforts of assassination directed against Florence MacCarthy, Hugh O'Neil, and the other Irish chieftains. The State Papers make strange revelations on this head. At one time we have an Englishman, in the pay of Sir Robert Cecyl, obtaining letters of introduction to the leading Jesuits in Ireland, and then with their commendation enrolling himself in the order of St. Francis, and all this that he might "get an opportunity of poisoning Hugh O'Neil." Another time, with the sanction and approval of her Majesty's Council, an assassin receives £10 from the Lord President of Munster, and being "furnished with a pistol out of the Queen's store, loaded by an experienced hand," sets out to murder John Fitz-Thomas, brother of the Earl of Desmond. Again, we have John Annyas set free from London Tower, and starting for Cork, with letters from her Majesty's ministers to administer poison to Florence MacCarthy.[2] And so in innumerable other cases. Indeed, the history of the policy of the English court towards Ireland, throughout the long reign of Elizabeth, may be traced in an endless series of such attempts at assassination and other legalized crimes of the deepest dye.

What a contrast is presented to us by the policy of the successor of St. Peter, who rules on the seven hills! Whilst Elizabeth was employing all her power against the Church of God, both at home and on the Continent, the agents of some great European powers suggested to the then reigning Pontiff, Sixtus V., that the hand of the assassin would without trouble rid the world of such a monster, but he indignantly spurned the suggestion: "He told Pisany," thus writes Baron Hubner, "that several times it had been proposed to him to assassinate her,

---

[1] "Of Marr the Regent, it has been said that he was too honest a man to pander to the jealousies or resentments of the English queen, and resolutely turned a deaf ear to the hints and suggestion of the envoy. Recent discoveries have, however, proved that, if at the first he affected to look upon the project as attended with difficulty and peril, he afterwards entered into it most cordially, and sought to drive a profitable bargain with Elizabeth."—*Lingard*, vi. 140. Full details of this assassination policy of the English Court, in reference to the Queen of Scots, will be found in "The Letter-Books of Sir Amias Poulet," edited by Rev. J. Morris, S.J. London, 1874.

[2] Extracts from the State Papers and other contemporary records, to illustrate the examples given in the text, will be found in the "Life and Letters of Florence MacCarthy Mor," by *Daniel MacCarthy*. London, 1867, pp. 286-307.

and for a small sum, but that he had rejected such proposals, detesting and abhorring means of that kind."[1]

5. And here a few words may not be out of place, as to a calumnious attack which has been rashly made against the memory of another great and holy Pope, St. Pius V. Lord Acton does not hesitate to write of that illustrious Pontiff: " Pius V., the only Pope who has been proclaimed a saint for many centuries, having deprived Elizabeth, commissioned an assassin to take her life." He was asked to assign his proofs for such an accusation, and in his reply he gives the case of Ridolfi as his only proof. Now the whole case of Ridolfi has been a long time well known to English historians, and yet not one of them has ever dared to ground on it such a charge against the cherished memory of Pope St. Pius V. We are told that even Elizabeth esteemed the virtues of that sainted Pontiff, and when he issued the sentence of excommunication against her, she stated that her only regret was, that it had proceeded from a Pope of such well known piety as Pius V.[2]

Ridolfi was an Italian merchant resident in London. The friends of Mary Stuart and the Duke of Norfolk chose him as their agent to solicit aid in men and arms from the Pope and from Philip II. of Spain. His chief commission, addressed to the Pope and the King of Spain, was signed by the Duke of Norfolk, a Protestant nobleman, then a prisoner in the Tower. It is published by Labanoff, and has not one syllable that even indirectly could be supposed to hint at the assassination of the Queen. Ridolfi was coldly received in Rome.[3] The Pontiff could not hold out a promise of the desired aid, but he wrote to Philip II. commending to his protection this mission of Ridolfi. The King of Spain smiled at the idea of such a commission being addressed to him by one who was a prisoner in Elizabeth's hands, and summoned Ridolfi to explain in person before his council what hopes could be entertained of success, and how far the friends of the Duke of Norfolk would be able on their part to co-operate with the troops of Spain. Ridolfi was so vague and extravagant in his statements, that Philip at once supposed him to be a secret agent of Elizabeth. It was on this occasion that Ridolfi spoke of a project which had been suggested by some friends of the imprisoned nobleman, to seize on the person of the Queen, and to keep her as a hostage for the safety of Mary Stuart, and if necessary to put her to death. So manifest was it, however, that this formed no part of his commission,

[1] *Hubner*, " Life of Sixtus V.," i. 350.   [3] *Bechetti*, xii. 108.
[2] *Lingard*, vi. 128.

that although the details of Ridolfi's interview with the Spanish council were quickly conveyed to Elizabeth, yet in the subsequent trials of the Duke of Norfolk and the Queen of Scots, and so many of her friends, no such commission was referred to, and no such project of assassination was laid to their charge. I will not detain you with further details on this subject. Suffice it to say, that in all the documents connected with Ridolfi, whether in the British Museum or at Simancas, there is not the slightest trace of any rumour or suspicion that the Pope had approved of a scheme of assassination ; no hint is even given that Ridolfi was himself an intended assassin, and much less is there to be found the shadow of a suspicion that " St. Pius V. commissioned an assassin to take the life of Elizabeth."

6. There are many other points on which it would be interesting to dwell in connection with the St. Bartholomew Massacre. But it is time that I should bring this tedious paper to a close ; and I trust that enough has been said to convince you that that terrible deed of blood was not decreed by the Holy See, nor carried into execution in the interests of the Catholic Church. The punishment which fell upon the Huguenots was a just retribution for their long career of conspiracies and assassinations, but it proceeded solely from the intrigues of the court, and was conformable to the false maxims of Protestant and Macchiavellian policy which then prevailed.

And now, in conclusion, allow me to congratulate you on the ardour with which you have entered on the historical pursuits of your Society, from which I trust that each one of you will derive the most abundant fruits. For three centuries history in these countries has been little more than a conspiracy against truth. You will, therefore, need great caution in accepting the statements of English historians, even when their statements seem to be only remotely connected with the Catholic Church, but much more so when they openly assail those illustrious Pontiffs who steered the bark of Peter amid the shoals and quicksands of the heresies that arose in the sixteenth century. Listen not to their assertions until you have closely examined them in the light of authentic contemporary records ; and even when supposed documents are presented to you, as sometimes happens, replete with calumnies against the Holy See, be still upon your guard ; accept them not on the word of anyone, no matter how eminent may be his name, but test their genuineness, and apply to them the critical rules which must be our guide in historical research. Take one instance to justify this counsel which I have given you. There was a class of men in the Italian schools of the seventeenth century, who being enamoured of the latitudinarian maxims which sprang up in the reformed sects, secretly bid adieu to morality and divine Faith, and became in their turn active propagandists of irreligion. One of the arts to which they had recourse in order to discredit the Holy See, which they instinctively recognised as the mainstay of religion and social order, was the following:—They invented a number of Papal Briefs and official despatches, in which the style of the supposed authors was carefully imitated, and dates were attached corresponding to the matters of which they treated. In these documents, copies of which were industriously circulated in the various schools of Italy and Germany, lying tales were told which had no foundation except in the wicked fancy of these propagandists of impiety; and it is to such sources that we may trace most of the charges which are repeated at the present day against some of our greatest Pontiffs. It is on such documents that the enemies of the Holy See rely; and yet, as a German historian, to whom I have already more than once referred, describes them: " They present to us mere idle fables which bear the print of vulgar ignorance, and resemble the popular tales which are generally told in Germany at country fairs, but notwithstanding their absurdity, eminent authors have actually reproduced them."[1]

[1] *Hübner*, " Life of Sixtus V.," vol. i., p. 15.

Browne and Nolan, Printers, Nassau-street, Dublin.

www.ingramcontent.com/pod-product-compliance
Lightning Source LLC
Chambersburg PA
CBHW031817090426
42739CB00008B/1318